A Robbie Reader

Meet Our New Student From

HAITI

John A. Torres

Mitchell Lane
PUBLISHERS

P.O. Box 196
Hockessin, Delaware 19707
Visit us on the web: www.mitchelllane.com
Comments? email us: mitchelllane@mitchelllane.com

Meet Our New Student From

Australia • China • Colombia • Great Britain • **Haiti** •
Israel • Korea • Malaysia • Mexico • New Zealand •
• Nigeria • Tanzania

Library of Congress Cataloging-in Publication Data to come.
Torres, John.
  Meet our new student from Haiti / by John Torres.
      p. cm.
  Includes bibliographical references and index.
  ISBN 978-1-58415-653-6 (library bound)
  1. Haiti—Juvenile literature. I. Title.
  F1915.2.T67 2008
  972.94--dc22
                                        2008002271

Printing 1   2   3   4   5   6   7   8   9

PLB

CONTENTS

Haiti

Even though Haiti is a beautiful country, there are very few opportunities to go to school and earn an education. Most people rely on natural resources for their survival.

Mr. Johns Makes an
Announcement

Chapter

On Friday afternoon, Mr. Johns said he had an announcement to make to our third-grade class at Dolphin Cove Elementary School. The school is in a little town called Indialantic (in-dee-ah-LAN-tik) in Florida. Indialantic is near a saltwater river and the ocean, so we see dolphins all the time.

The other kids in the class groaned because usually, when Mr. Johns makes a Friday announcement, it's to tell us we have a big homework assignment over the weekend. I was playing in a soccer tournament over the weekend, so I was hoping it wasn't about homework.

"Class, I have a weekend homework assignment for you." Mr. Johns smiled. "No, no, quiet down," he continued. "This is going to be fun. We have a new student starting class here on Monday, and he is not

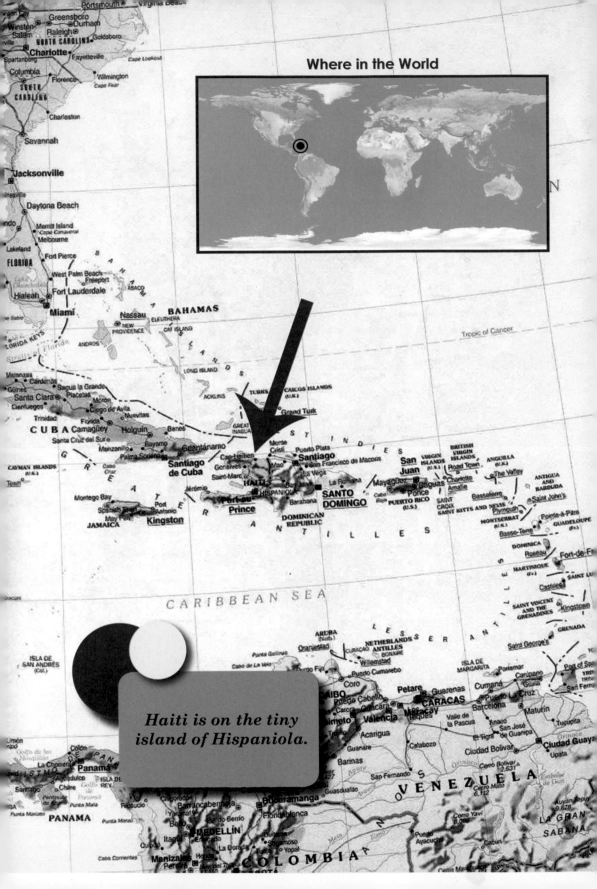

Where in the World

Haiti is on the tiny island of Hispaniola.

from the United States. I want all of you to go to the library or use the Internet to find out as much about his country as you can. We want to make him feel as comfortable as possible. It can be scary starting school in a new place."

"Mr. Johns," I said, raising my hand.

"Yes, Robbie. What is it?" he answered.

"Aren't you forgetting something?"

"I don't think so."

"Where is he from?" I asked.

"Ah, I guess I did forget something very important. His name is Jean Paul Petit and he is from a small country called Haiti." He said the kid's name like *JHON Pawl PEH-tee,* from *HAY-tee.*

Mr. Johns walked over to the blackboard and pulled down a huge map of the world. There were little stickers all over the map, showing where Mr. Johns had been. He used to be in the Air Force, so he had been to a lot of countries.

He used the pointer to show us Florida. Then he moved the pointer down past Cuba, and then to the right a little bit. He stopped it on a small island.

"This little dot on the map is called Hispaniola [his-pan-YOH-luh]," he said. "Haiti is one of two countries on Hispaniola."

Chapter 1

FACTS ABOUT HAITI

Total Area: 10,714 square miles (about the size of Massachusetts)
Population: 8,706,500 (2007 estimate)
Capital City: Port-au-Prince
Languages: French, Creole (official languages)

Religions: Roman Catholic, Protestant (people in these groups may also practice voodoo)
Chief Exports: Coffee, mangoes, sugarcane, rice, corn, sorghum; wood
Monetary Unit: Gourdes

That's when all the kids in the class raised their hands with a question.

"*Hispaniola* sounds like Spanish," said Margaret, the smartest girl in the class. "Do they speak Spanish in Haiti?"

"That's a great question, Margaret," Mr. Johns said. "Some people from Haiti speak Spanish, but most of them speak French or Creole [KREE-ohl]."

Haiti is near the equator in the Caribbean Sea.

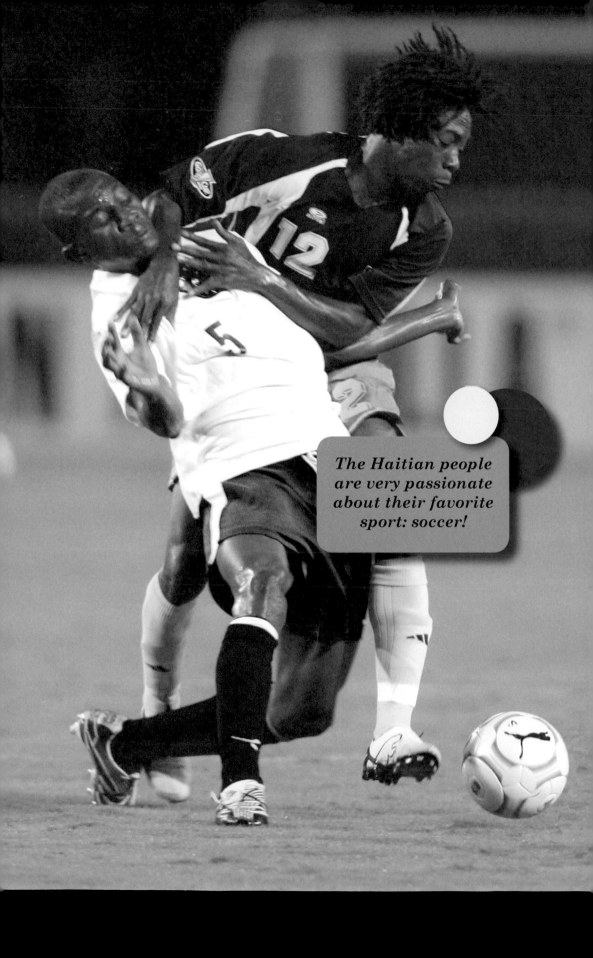

The Haitian people are very passionate about their favorite sport: soccer!

Another kid asked what Creole was. I had never heard of it either.

Mr. Johns explained that it was sort of like a simple form of French with a little Spanish and African thrown in.

"But Haiti is far away from Africa," I called out. Then I realized I had never been so excited about homework before.

By the end of the day, Mr. Johns had filled us in on some of the basics. The people from Haiti are called Haitians (HAY-shuns). Many of their great-great-great-great grandfathers were taken from Africa to Haiti as slaves.

Haitians eat a lot of rice, beans, vegetables, and fruit. Their country is very poor, and mudslides and floods sometimes kill hundreds of people a year. Not every Haitian kid is lucky enough to go to school.

Avocados are grown in Haiti.

And then I heard something that really made me excited.

"Their favorite sport," Mr. Johns said, "is soccer."

Haiti

Many visitors to Haiti, especially those on cruise ships, never see the poverty of one of the world's poorest countries. Labadee is a port located on the northern coast. It is a private resort used by one of the major cruise companies.

A Brief History of
Haiti

Chapter 2

Haiti is on the Caribbean (kuh-RIH-bee-un) island of Hispaniola. It shares the island with the country of the Dominican Republic (doh-MIH-nih-kun ree-PUB-lik).

Before there were ever any Haitians or Dominicans on the island, the Taino Arawak (TY-noh AA-ruh-wok) people lived there. Because of all the mountains on the island, the Taino called the island *Ayiti*. This word means "mountain land" and sounds a lot like the present-day pronunciation of *Haiti*.

The same explorer who discovered America—Christopher Columbus—also found Hispaniola. His ships landed on the island on December 5, 1492. Columbus was Italian, but he was working for the country of Spain. He claimed Hispaniola for the Kingdom of Spain.

A few weeks later, while exploring the **coastline**, one of his ships—the *Santa María*—got stuck in an

Christopher Columbus

area that would be known as Cap-Haitien in northern Haiti. Columbus left behind about forty men to make the first Spanish settlement in the land.

Over the years, more and more Spaniards moved to Haiti. They accidentally brought with them a lot of diseases, like smallpox, that would kill a large number of the native people. Looking for workers to build roads, houses, forts, and ships, the Spanish began to bring over people from West Africa. They used these people as slaves.

In the 1600s, the Spanish were putting all their efforts on Hispaniola into settling the eastern part of the island. Soon the French took over the western third—the part that is now Haiti. In 1697, that part officially became a French **colony**.

Haiti is known for growing things like sugarcane, the plant from which sugar is harvested. Sugarcane is cut in long stalks and then processed for its sweet insides.

The French discovered that their new colony could make them a lot of money. They began exporting

Coffee beans are also grown in Haiti. Haitian coffee is sold in specialty shops and Caribbean grocers around the world.

large amounts of sugar and coffee. It soon became the richest colony in the western **hemisphere** (HEH-mis-feer).

The Citadel is a large mountaintop fortress located in northern Haiti. It is the largest fortress in the western hemisphere.

By the late 1700s, there were many more slaves than French nationals living in the colony, and the slaves were treated very badly. A black man, François-Dominique Toussaint L'Ouverture (too-SAN LOO-vuhtyur), led the slaves in a war against the French and defeated them.

On January 1, 1804, Haiti became an **independent** country. The new government quickly grew to be one of the world leaders against the use of slavery. In fact, many people credit the slave revolt in Haiti for slave rebellions in other countries, including those in the United States.

fun FACTS

Haiti is the third largest country in the Caribbean. Second is the Dominican Republic, which shares the island of Hispaniola with Haiti. Cuba is the largest country there.

In 1806, the government of Haiti collapsed. The island was run as two different countries—north and south—for a few years. It reunited for good as the Republic of Haiti in 1820.

For much of the twentieth and into the twenty-first century, Haiti has suffered through shaky leadership,

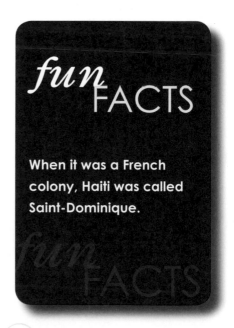

fun FACTS

When it was a French colony, Haiti was called Saint-Dominique.

Popular hip-hop singer Wyclef Jean (left) attends a dinner with Rene Preval, the president of Haiti. Wyclef Jean was born in Haiti.

corrupt governments, and military takeovers. In 2004, President Jean-Bertrand Aristide was ousted from power in a violent revolt. After special elections were finally held in 2006, Rene Preval was named president.

Haiti

Even though Haiti's climate is tropical and most of the vegetation is closer to a jungle than a desert, you can still find cactus plants throughout the island of Hispaniola.

The Land

Chapter **3**

Hispaniola is an island of mountain ranges. The Haitian portion of Hispaniola juts out into two **peninsulas**. One points toward its neighbor to the west, Jamaica, and the other toward its neighbor to the northwest, Cuba. To the south of Haiti, across the Caribbean Sea, are the South American countries of Colombia and Venezuela.

Located much closer to the equator than any part of the United States, Haiti is considered tropical. The year-round average temperature is 80°F, but it is in the 90s for a good part of the year.

The rugged and steep mountains are what helped the rebel slave army defeat the French in the battle for independence. The French were not used to traveling on those narrow roads and high hills. But those same

A schoolboy in Haiti uses a donkey to fetch sand and rocks from the hillside. He will take them back to a construction site where a new school is being built.

mountains have also made life hard for the poor people of Haiti.

In the mornings, even before it gets light, the mountain roads are filled with people walking toward the cities down below. There, farmers sell mangoes, bananas, and other kinds of produce. In many places, it takes the people hours to walk down the mountains and hours to go back up later.

Because it is so difficult to travel the mountain roads, the people who live in the rural mountain villages are **isolated** (EYE-soh-lay-ted). Far from major cities, they have no electricity, no plumbing, and no television. Many areas do not even have a school. With few jobs and little education, it is very difficult for Haitians to improve their **economy** (ee-KAH-nuh-mee).

The mountains can also be very dangerous for the people who live down below. The main source of

*fun*FACTS

Some of Haiti's natural resources are copper, gold, marble, and hydropower (electricity from rushing water).

*fun*FACTS

In 2008, almost 1.8 million people were living in Haiti's capital, Port-au-Prince. That was 20 percent of the country's entire population.

A Haitian farmer uses large wagons to move his crops of hay. The people of Haiti have to work very hard for very little money.

fuel in Haiti comes from charcoal, which is made by cutting down trees and burning the wood. When coffee and sugar prices dropped in the 1960s, many Haitian farmers began making and selling charcoal. They cut down many trees, which has led to soil **erosion** (ee-ROH-zhun). Now there are not enough trees to

More than 1,000 people died in Tropical Storm Jeanne in 2004. Deforestation in Haiti has led to deadly flash floods and mudslides during heavy rains.

hold back water when it rains. As a result, mudslides and flash floods have killed thousands of Haitians. Some of the world's major scientists have called the situation in Haiti an **environmental** (en-vy-run-MEN-tul) crisis.

A satellite photograph of Port-au-Prince, an important city in Haiti. Besides being the capital, Port-au-Prince is a seaport. Many trade goods enter and leave Haiti through this city.

The capital and largest city in Haiti is a seaport called Port-au-Prince. The views from Port-au-Prince are beautiful, but the city is also one of the poorest and most violent in the Caribbean. Haiti's government and

In Port-au-Prince, the houses are very small and close together.
Most of the people who live there are poor.

police force have been unable to stop the violence
and kidnappings in the capital. Since 2006, soldiers
from the United Nations have patrolled the streets in
tanks and armored vehicles to maintain peace.

Many Haitians looking for a better way of life have left the island on small boats bound for the United States. If they are caught by the U.S. Coast Guard, they are sent back.

Religion, Customs, Culture

Chapter

In the quiet woods just beyond the mountain villages, hours before the sun comes up and the first rooster begins to crow, you can sometimes hear drums. These are not the kinds of drums used by American rock-and-roll bands, but bongo and conga drums, beating rhythmically for hours.

These drums were common in Africa. They have been part of Haitian culture and religion for hundreds of years. If you ask people why the drums are playing, they may tell you different things. Even though nearly 100 percent of Haitians are Christian, with 80 percent being Roman Catholic, just about everyone practices voodoo. The drums are voodoo drums.

Voodoo is based on African religions that use sorcery, witchcraft, and **superstition** to call upon certain spirits. Because voodoo and Christian beliefs

do not logically go together, people in Haiti do not admit to practicing voodoo, and they do it secretly.

The midnight drums are some of the evidence that it does occur.

The author asked Father Yves Anis (EEV ah-NEEZ), a Catholic priest in the small mountain town of Morne à Chandelle, about the drums. "Oh, those were just people practicing for Mother's Day," Father Anis answered. Then he winked.

Haitian culture is a mix of West African, French, and Caribbean cultures. The official languages are French and Haitian Creole. More and more people, however, are learning to speak Spanish in order to communicate (kuh-MYOO-nih-kayt) with people from the Dominican Republic. Also, people in many other countries in the

fun FACTS

Many Haitians claim that the merengue musical style originated in Haiti and not the Dominican Republic.

Kindergarten students color during school. Because there is very little space in the school, many classes are held outdoors. Each student receives only one piece of paper from a coloring book and only one crayon at a time. They share their crayons.

area, including Cuba, Venezuela, and Puerto Rico, speak Spanish.

The children who are lucky enough to go to school are treated with a day that is in some ways similar to the school day in the United States. In other ways, it is very different. Kids walk for miles and miles to Father

Students start every school day by raising the national flag, singing the national anthem, and saying a prayer. These students attend a small Catholic school in the mountains. The teachers walk about five miles from their homes.

Anis's school. They leave very early in order to make it there by eight in the morning. (The teachers have to walk miles and miles too!)

Then all the students, from kindergarten on up, sit quietly in their seats, waiting to eat breakfast. The small school buildings have open-air windows, no lights, and old rickety chairs. The younger students sit in smaller chairs outside the building. Breakfast is a peanut butter sandwich. Not one student will eat until all 300 children have their food in front of them.

After eating, the students attend a short assembly, where they raise the flag of Haiti, sing their national anthem, and then say a prayer. After that the learning begins. This part of the school day might sound familiar to a student in the United States. In Haiti, the kids study arithmetic, reading, writing, and French language. And of course, in the middle of the day, there is recess! But unlike in the

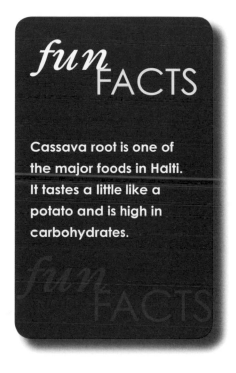

fun FACTS

Cassava root is one of the major foods in Haiti. It tastes a little like a potato and is high in carbohydrates.

United States, there is no playground or playground equipment. The kids all kick around a soccer ball for fun.

The people in Haiti, though they are very poor, are eager to smile and have a good time. They love to sing and dance. They hold many festivals and

The religion of voodoo involves many rituals and celebrations. It also yields artwork like crafts, paintings, and masks.

celebrations throughout the year, such as Carnival, Rara, and Drapo art celebrations. The typical music of Haiti is called Kompa, which means "rhythm" or "tone." It mixes Cuban-African sounds with horns or electronic **synthesizers** (SIN-theh-sy-zurs).

By 2008, a Haitian hip-hop, reggae, Creole music superstar named Wyclef Jean (WY-klef JEEN) had become very popular around the world. He was born in Croix-des-Bouquets, Haiti, in 1972. When he was nine years old, his family moved to Brooklyn, New York. He began playing the guitar and studying different kinds of music, like hip-hop, jazz, and rock. In the late 1980s, he formed the Fugees (short for Refugees). The group was very successful, but eventually all three members left to start solo careers.

Even though Wyclef has enjoyed a great career in the United States, he has never forgotten his Haitian roots. In 2004 he recorded an album called *Welcome to Haiti: Creole 101*. On the album, he sings much of the songs in Creole.

He has also done a lot of charity work for his native country. He started a foundation called Yéle Haiti. The purpose of the group is to improve education, health, and the environment in Haiti. Some Yéle volunteers clean the streets of Port-au-Prince. Others work to provide clean drinking water for the people.

In Haiti, just about everyone knows who Wyclef Jean is.

Although the waters around Haiti are full of fish, the country does not have a real commercial fishing industry.

J.P.'s First Day of
School

Chapter

I called Mr. Johns over the weekend with an idea. He agreed to help me with my plan, and together we called all the students in the class, asking them to arrive ten minutes early on Monday. We wanted to make sure we were there before Jean Paul arrived.

We put a few of our desks together and set out our feast. There was a platter of yellow rice with beans, some steamed red cabbage, a bowl of tassot, and bread with spicy peanut butter.

Just before the eight o'clock bell rang, a shy, skinny boy wearing baggy blue jeans, sandals, and wire-rimmed glasses that kept slipping down his nose walked slowly into the dark classroom.

On the count of three, we all jumped up and yelled, *"Bonjou. Kouman ou ye? Ki non ou?"*

Haitians eat many types of root vegetables with their meals, including cassava and carrots.

It was my idea to get the whole class to learn how to say, "Good morning. How are you? What is your name?" in Creole, Jean Paul's native language.

His face went from shy to a big smile. He started waving to us and exclaimed: *"Bonjou! Non pa'm se Jean Paul."* Then he laughed. "But you can call me J.P."

We all shared our Haitian treats, and then we went around the room telling J.P. all the things we had learned about Haiti over the last few days. Mr. Johns asked J.P. to tell us a little bit about his life.

He had gone to school for one year, but then had to stop so that he could help his parents grow sugarcane on their small mountain farm. Some kids said he was lucky, but then his face grew serious.

> ### *fun* FACTS
> As new schools are being built in the mountains of Haiti, people are going to school for the first time. It is not uncommon for a young student to be the first in his family ever to go to school.

"No," he said. "You are the lucky ones. In my country, everyone wants to go to school, but not many of us can. How can I become a doctor if I don't go to school?"

Chapter 5

Jean Paul showed us a picture of him (middle) with his little sister and some friends. In Haiti, children need a uniform to go to school. Sometimes they have to share uniforms with their brothers or sisters, so they cannot attend school every day.

He told us about some relatives who lived in Miami. They were able to sponsor his family with visas to enter the country. A visa is a piece of paper that allows someone from one country to enter another country.

By the time recess rolled around, I felt like I was an expert on Haiti. Then I reached into my backpack for my soccer ball and showed it to my new friend.

"Come on," he said, picking up our English pretty quickly. "Let's go play."

How To Make
Tassot

Recipe

Tassot is a traditional Haitian meal of fried goat or beef. It is very simple to make.

Instructions

1. In a large bowl, combine all the ingredients except the oil. Let the ingredients marinate in the refrigerator for at least three hours.

2. Pour the meat mixture into a cooking pot. Add a little bit of water and let it boil for about an hour, until it is tender.

3. **Ask an adult** to heat the oil in a frying pan. Fry for about three minutes, until it is crisp.

Things You Will Need

Large bowl
Cooking pot
Frying pan
Refrigerator
An adult to help you

Ingredients

2 pounds of goat or beef, cut into small chunks

½ cup orange juice

¼ cup lime juice

1 teaspoon parsley

a pinch each of salt and pepper

½ cup vegetable oil

Make Your Own
Coconut Shell Nativity Set

You Will Need

an adult

1 whole coconut

knife

spoon

2 bowls

5-6 small pieces of wood
(or clay)

sandpaper

paint

paintbrush

Instructions For Making
A Coconut Shell Nativity Set

1 **Ask an adult** to cut a fresh coconut in half. Let the coconut milk drain into one bowl.

2 Scrape the meat out of the shell and into a second bowl. Refrigerate the milk and coconut meat—you can eat them later. Leave the shell out to dry.

3 Find five or six small pieces of wood and, using sandpaper, smooth out all the edges until they are the size of an adult's thumb.

4 Paint the figures black.

5 Once the black paint is dry, paint faces and clothes on your pieces.

6 Store the figures in the empty coconut shell, using both halves to keep it closed.

Coconut Shell Doll Houses or Nativity Sets

Many Haitian children paint Nativity sets because the country is largely Christian. A Nativity set shows baby Jesus in the manger, surrounded by his mother, Mary, his father, Joseph, and the shepherds and animals that were in the barn where he was born. You can make figures for a Nativity set, or any other figures you'd like.

Further Reading

Books

Arthur, Charles. *Haiti in Focus: A Guide to the People, Politics, and Culture*. Northampton, Massachusetts: Interlink Publishing Group, 2002.

Bontemps, Arna, and Langston Hughes. *Popo and Fifina: Children of Haiti*. New York, Oxford Press, 2000.

Goldstein, Margaret J. *Haiti in Pictures*. Minneapolis, Minnesota: Lerner Publishing Group, 2006.

Shapiro, Norma, and Jayme Adelson-Goldstein. *The Oxford Picture Dictionary: English-Haitian Creole Edition*. New York: Oxford University Press, 1999.

Wolkstein, Diane, and Jesse Sweetwater (illustrator). *Bouki Dances the Kokioko: A Comical Tale from Haiti*. New York: Harcourt, 1997.

Embassy

Embassy of the Republic of Haiti
2311 Massachusetts Avenue, N.W.
Washington, D.C. 20008
Tel: 202-332-4090
Fax: 202-745-7215
E-mail: embassy@haiti.org
http://www.haiti.org

Sources

Author John Torres has made several trips to Haiti and the Dominican Republic to cover disasters and disaster relief in those countries. This book was written from his personal experiences there, and from information in the following sources.

Personal trip to Haiti, 2007

Personal trip to Haiti and Jimani, Dominican Republic, 2004

BBC News Country Profile: Haiti
http//news.bbc.co

Central Intelligence Agency: The World Factbook: Haiti
www.cia.gov

Embassy of the Republic of Haiti in Washington D.C.
www.haiti.org

Opportunities to Help in Haiti (Father Yves Anis)
http://home.cfl.rr.com/hnjhaiti/pages/current.html

Wyclef Jean Official Website
www.wyclef.com

Yéle Haiti
www.yele.org

Glossary

coastline (KOHST-lyn)—The shore along an ocean.

colony (KAH-luh-nee)—An area that has ties to a larger state or country.

economy (ee-KAH-nuh-mee)—The flow of goods and money.

environmental (en-vy-run-MEN-tul)—Dealing with soil, water, air, and living things.

erosion (ee-ROH-zhun)—The wearing away by water or wind.

hemisphere (HEH-mis-feer)—Half a sphere, such as half of planet Earth.

independent (in-dee-PEN-dent)—Having the power to self-govern.

isolated (EYE-soh-lay-ted)—Cut off from other places where people live.

peninsula (peh-NIN-soo-luh)—A narrow portion of land with water on three sides.

superstition (soo-per-STIH-shun)—Fear of the unknown, or a belief in magic.

synthesizers (SIN-theh-sy-zurs)—Computerized musical instruments.

Index

ABOUT THE AUTHOR

John A. Torres is an award-winning newspaper reporter from Central Florida. His stories have taken him to Africa, Italy, Indonesia, Mexico, India, and Haiti. In 2004 he traveled to the Dominican Republic village of Jimani, where devastating mudslides had killed 3,000 people. It was there—and just west of the border—that he met and learned for the first time the hardships of the Haitian people.

Torres returned to Haiti in April 2007 with his wife, Jennifer, and several members of their church on a mission of mercy. He hopes to make it an annual event.

Torres is the author of more than 40 children's books, including many titles for Mitchell Lane Publishers.